Little People, **BIG DREAMS**

MAYA ANGELOU

Little People, **BIG DREAMS**

MAYA ANGELOU

Written by
Lisbeth Kaiser

Illustrated by
Leire Salaberria

Frances Lincoln
Children's Books

Marguerite was born in the city of St. Louis, U.S.A. Her brother called her Maya. When Maya was four, she and her brother were sent to live with their grandmother in Stamps, Arkansas.

Growing up in the South, Maya was treated unfairly because of the colour of her skin and because she was a girl. The world outside was very cruel.

Home was hard too. When Maya was eight, her mother's boyfriend attacked her. Maya was so upset, she stopped talking.

A friend of her grandmother's named Mrs Flowers noticed that Maya was afraid to use her voice. Mrs Flowers showed Maya all kinds of wonderful books, and how the words come alive when you read them out loud.

Maya found her voice again in the stories and poems of great writers. She loved words so much, she read every book in the library.

Even though Maya was a great student, she was told that she couldn't get a good job because of the colour of her skin.

"lift ever

But she had pride and hope. She thought,
"There's nothing I can't be."

voice "

And she was right.
She was a cook and a streetcar conductor.

She was a dancer, a singer and an actress.

She travelled the world, and learned to speak a lot of languages.

At home in America, she worked to
help all people get treated equally.

It wasn't until Maya was all grown up that
she decided she wanted to be a writer.
So she began writing a book about her life.

She told the story of a little girl who struggled through hard times but didn't give up.

People all around the world were moved by her powerful story and her beautiful words.

Maya became a famous writer, teacher and speaker, inspiring everyone with her belief that you can be anything you want to be.

On the day Bill Clinton became president, Maya read a poem. She had once been a little girl who was afraid to use her voice. Now she was speaking to the entire country, about her favourite thing: hope.

MAYA ANGELOU

(Born 1928 • Died 2014)

1937

1957

Maya Angelou is one of the most memorable voices in American culture. Born Marguerite Annie Johnson in St. Louis, Missouri, she spent much of her childhood in a small town in the South. There, she faced a lot of unfairness because of her skin colour. When she was eight, she was attacked by her mother's boyfriend and she stopped speaking for five years. In that time, she grew to love books and found power and strength in words. Maya overcame her childhood struggles and went on to lead a marvellous life. She became a dancer, singer, actress, writer, director, journalist, playwright, producer, teacher and an activist

1971   1990

for civil rights. She performed in nightclubs, and began calling herself Maya Angelou. She also became a mother and a grandmother. In 1969, Maya turned the memories from her childhood into a book called *I Know Why the Caged Bird Sings*. The book became famous and sold millions of copies around the world. Maya wrote many more books, won many awards and read her poems at the White House and the United Nations. People everywhere continue to be inspired by her incredible life, her beautiful words and her powerful, hopeful voice.

Want to find out more about **Maya Angelou**?

She has written many great books herself, like:
Poetry for Young People: Maya Angelou edited by Dr. Edwin Graves Wilson
Ph.D, illustrated by Jerome Lagarrigue

You could also try these biographies:
Who Was Maya Angelou? by Ellen Labrecque, Dede Putra and Nancy Harrison
Maya Angelou: Journey of the Heart by Jayne Pettit

Brimming with creative inspiration, how-to projects, and useful information to enrich your everyday life, Quarto Knows is a favourite destination for those pursuing their interests and passions. Visit our site and dig deeper with our books into your area of interest: Quarto Creates, Quarto Cooks, Quarto Homes, Quarto Lives, Quarto Drives, Quarto Explores, Quarto Gifts, or Quarto Kids.

First published in the UK and the US in 2016 by Frances Lincoln Children's Books,
an imprint of the Quarto Group.
The Old Brewery, 6 Blundell Street, London N7 9BH
Visit our blogs at QuartoKnows.com

Commissioned as part of the Little People, Big Dreams series,
conceived by Mª Isabel Sánchez Vegara.
Originally published under the title Pequeña & Grande by Alba Editorial (www.albaeditorial.es)
Translation rights arranged by IMC Literary Agency

Maya Angelou™ is a trademark of Caged Bird Legacy, LLC. MayaAngelou.com
Text copyright © 2016 by Lisbeth Kaiser
Illustrations copyright © 2016 by Leire Salaberria

A catalogue record for this book is available from the British Library.

ISBN 978-1-84780-890-5

Manufactured in Guangdong, China, CC082020

13

Photographic acknowledgements (pages 28-29, from left to right) 1. Photo and Maya Angelou™ is a trademark of Caged Bird Legacy, LLC. MayaAngelou.com 2. Photo © Everett Collection Historical / Alamy Stock Photo 3. Photo © ASSOCIATED PRESS 4. Photo by: Universal History Archive/UIG via Getty images

Collect the
Little People, **BIG DREAMS** series:

FRIDA KAHLO

ISBN: 978-1-84780-770-0

COCO CHANEL

ISBN: 978-1-84780-771-7

MAYA ANGELOU

ISBN: 978-1-84780-890-5

AMELIA EARHART

ISBN: 978-1-84780-885-1

AGATHA CHRISTIE

ISBN: 978-1-84780-959-9

MARIE CURIE

ISBN: 978-1-84780-961-2

ROSA PARKS

ISBN: 978-1-78603-017-7

AUDREY HEPBURN

ISBN: 978-1-78603-052-8

EMMELINE PANKHURST

ISBN: 978-1-78603-019-1

ELLA FITZGERALD

ISBN: 978-1-78603-086-3

ADA LOVELACE

ISBN: 978-1-78603-075-7

JANE AUSTEN

ISBN: 978-1-78603-119-8

GEORGIA O'KEEFFE

ISBN: 978-1-78603-121-1

HARRIET TUBMAN

ISBN: 978-1-78603-289-8

ANNE FRANK

ISBN: 978-1-78603-292-8

MOTHER TERESA

ISBN: 978-1-78603-290-4

JOSEPHINE BAKER

ISBN: 978-1-78603-291-1

L. M. MONTGOMERY

ISBN: 978-1-78603-295-9

JANE GOODALL

ISBN: 978-1-78603-294-2

SIMONE DE BEAUVOIR

ISBN: 978-1-78603-293-5

MUHAMMAD ALI

ISBN: 978-1-78603-733-6

STEPHEN HAWKING

ISBN: 978-1-78603-732-9

MARIA MONTESSORI

ISBN: 978-1-78603-753-4

VIVIENNE WESTWOOD

ISBN: 978-1-78603-756-5

MAHATMA GANDHI

ISBN: 978-1-78603-334-5

DAVID BOWIE

ISBN: 978-1-78603-803-6

WILMA RUDOLPH

ISBN: 978-1-78603-750-3

DOLLY PARTON

ISBN: 978-1-78603-759-6

BRUCE LEE

ISBN: 978-1-78603-335-2

RUDOLF NUREYEV

ISBN: 978-1-78603-336-9

ZAHA HADID

ISBN: 978-1-78603-744-2

MARY SHELLEY

ISBN: 978-1-78603-747-3

MARTIN LUTHER KING JR.

ISBN: 978-0-7112-4566-2

DAVID ATTENBOROUGH

ISBN: 978-0-7112-4563-1

ASTRID LINDGREN

ISBN: 978-1-78603-762-6

EVONNE GOOLAGONG

ISBN: 978-0-7112-4585-3

BOB DYLAN

ISBN: 978-0-7112-4674-4

ALAN TURING

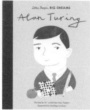

ISBN: 978-0-7112-4677-5

BILLIE JEAN KING

ISBN: 978-0-7112-4692-8

GRETA THUNBERG

ISBN: 978-0-7112-5643-9

JESSE OWENS

ISBN: 978-0-7112-4582-2

JEAN-MICHEL BASQUIAT

ISBN: 978-0-7112-4579-2

ARETHA FRANKLIN

ISBN: 978-0-7112-4687-4

CORAZON AQUINO

ISBN: 978-0-7112-4683-6

PELÉ

ISBN: 978-0-7112-4574-7

ERNEST SHACKLETON

ISBN: 978-0-7112-4570-9

STEVE JOBS

ISBN: 978-0-7112-4576-1

AYRTON SENNA

ISBN: 978-0-7112-4671-3

LOUISE BOURGEOIS

ISBN: 978-0-7112-4689-8

ELTON JOHN

ISBN: 978-0-7112-5838-9